LIVING IN THE WILD: PRIMATES

CHIMPANZEES

Heidi Moore

Heinemann
LIBRARY

Chicago, Illinois

www.capstonepub.com
Visit our website to find out more information about Heinemann-Raintree books.

To order:
☎ Phone 888-454-2279
💻 Visit www.capstonepub.com
  to browse our catalog and order online.

Edited by Abby Colich, Jilly Hunt, and Vaarunika Dharmapala
Designed by Victoria Allen
Picture research by Tracy Cummins
Original illustrations © Capstone Global Library Ltd 2012
Illustrations by Oxford Designers & Illustrators and HL Studios

Originated by Capstone Global Library Ltd
Printed and bound in China by CTPS

15 14 13 12 11
10 9 8 7 6 5 4 3 2 1

Library of Congress Cataloging-in-Publication Data
Moore, Heidi.
  Chimpanzees / Heidi Moore.—1st ed.
    p. cm.—(Living in the wild: primates)
  Includes bibliographical references and index.
  ISBN 978-1-4329-5862-6 (hb)—ISBN 978-1-4329-5869-5 (pb) 1. Chimpanzees—Juvenile literature. I. Title.
  QL737.P96M67 2012
  599.885—dc22   2011012892

Acknowledgments
We would like to thank the following for permission to reproduce photographs: AP Photo p. 36 (PRNewsFoto/CareerBuilder.com); FLPA pp. 4 (Frans Lanting), 6 (Jurgen & Christine Sohns), 9 (Frans Lanting), 11 (Frans Lanting), 14 (Frans Lanting), 19 (Cyril Ruoso/Minden Pictures), 21 (Frans Lanting), 22 (Frans Lanting), 29 (Cyril Ruoso/Minden Pictures), 30 (Cyril Ruoso/Minden Pictures), 44 (Frans Lanting); Getty Images pp. 31 (Altrendo Images), 41 (David S. Holloway); Newscom pp. 26 (Lu Chuanquan/Xinhua/Photoshot), 35 (ZUMA Press), 39 (ZUMA Press); Photolibrary pp. 15 (Cyril Ruoso), 23 (Clive Bromhall), 24 (Michel Gunther), 33 (Stan Osolinski), 42 (Martin Harvey); Photoshot pp. 27 (Marc Mueller), 34 (NHPA/Daniel Heuclin); Shutterstock pp. 7 (© Uryadnikov Sergey), 12 (© Sam Dcruz), 13 (© Uryadnikov Sergey), 17 (© Sam Dcruz), 25 (© Uryadnikov Sergey), 38 (© Ewan Chesser), 40 (© Morgan Lane Photography), 43 (© Uryadnikov Sergey).

Cover photograph of a chimpanzee at Nambe Island Chimpanzee Sanctuary, Uganda, reproduced with permission of Photolibrary (Sue Flood).

Every effort has been made to contact copyright holders of any material reproduced in this book. Any omissions will be rectified in subsequent printings if notice is given to the publisher.

Contents

Some words are shown in bold, **like this**. You can find out what they mean by looking in the glossary.

What Are Primates?

Deep in the **rain forest** of Tanzania, you spy a chimpanzee in the thick leaves. It glides through the trees, swinging from branch to branch. Suddenly, she decides to stop. She leaps down from the tree and lands on two feet. Then she begins to search the ground carefully. She is on the hunt for food: some ripe berries, or perhaps some bird eggs that have fallen from a tree.

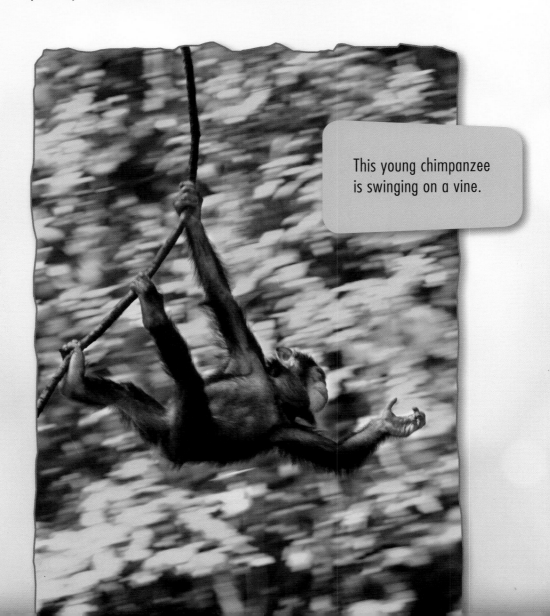

This young chimpanzee is swinging on a vine.

Chimpanzees, monkeys, and you!

A chimpanzee is a primate. Primates are a type of **mammal**. Mammals have hair, give birth to live young, and feed their young milk from their bodies. Monkeys, lemurs, gorillas, orangutans, and bonobos are all primates. Humans are primates, too. Yes, you are a primate!

There are more than 350 **species** of primates. They all have hands that can grasp, eyes that face forward, and flat nails on their hands and feet. Having eyes that face forward gives them better vision. Female primates usually give birth to one baby at a time. Primates also have large brains compared to their body size. This makes them very intelligent.

This map shows where in the world non-human primates live.

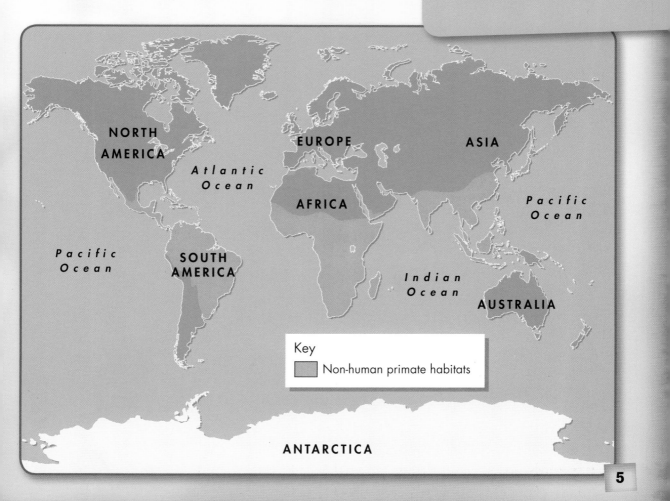

NORTH AMERICA

EUROPE

ASIA

Atlantic Ocean

AFRICA

Pacific Ocean

Pacific Ocean

SOUTH AMERICA

Indian Ocean

AUSTRALIA

Key

Non-human primate habitats

ANTARCTICA

What Are Chimpanzees?

Have you ever seen a chimpanzee? You have probably seen them at the zoo, in books, or on television. Chimps are amazing animals to watch. They have very expressive faces. They pout when begging for food, bare their teeth when angry, and grin when excited or afraid.

Chimpanzees are slightly smaller than humans. They stand 3 feet to 5 feet, 6 inches (1 meter to 1.7 meters) tall and weigh 70 to 130 pounds (32 to 60 kilograms). The largest chimps are about the size of a small adult human.

Chimps have brown or black hair all over their bodies and hairless faces with short beards. Even female chimps have beards. Beneath their hairy coats, chimps may have pale white-ish or brown skin. Their face, hands, and feet range from pink to dark brown. Male chimpanzees are larger than females.

This adult male chimpanzee is standing upright.

Great apes

Chimpanzees, bonobos, gorillas, and orangutans belong to a group called great apes. Great apes share many characteristics and live in similar **habitats**. They live in African **rain forests**, woodlands, and grasslands.

Great apes also share many things with humans. In fact, they share most of our **DNA**. DNA determines everything from the color of your hair to whether you can roll your tongue. Chimpanzees and bonobos are the animals closest to humans. They share more than 98 percent of our DNA.

COMMON ANCESTRY

Chimps and humans come from a common ancestor. At some point between 4.6 and 6.2 million years ago, this animal branched off into chimps and humans.

These orangutans belong to the group called great apes, just as chimpanzees do.

7

How Are Chimpanzees Classified?

Classifying things is the way that humans try to make sense of the living world. Grouping living things together by the characteristics that they share allows us to identify them and understand why they live where they do and behave as they do.

Classification is important because there are so many different **species** of living thing. The total number of species may be as many as 100 million!

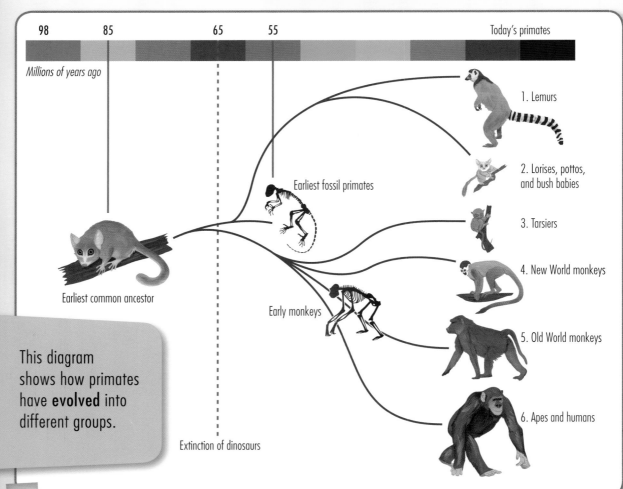

| 98 | 85 | | 65 | 55 | | Today's primates |

Millions of years ago

Earliest fossil primates

1. Lemurs

2. Lorises, pottos, and bush babies

3. Tarsiers

4. New World monkeys

Earliest common ancestor

Early monkeys

5. Old World monkeys

6. Apes and humans

This diagram shows how primates have **evolved** into different groups.

Extinction of dinosaurs

Classification groups

There are seven standard animal classification groups. These are kingdom, phylum, class, order, family, genus, and species. Sometimes, further classification involves adding more groups, such as a subspecies. Each of the standard groups contains fewer and fewer members. For example, there are far more animals to be found in the class Mammalia (**mammals**) than in the genus *Pan* (chimpanzees and bonobos).

Classification of chimpanzees

There is only one main species of chimpanzee. However, there are three subspecies of chimpanzee: the Central African chimpanzee, the West African chimpanzee, and the East African chimpanzee.

All three chimpanzee subspecies look very similar, although the East African chimp has longer, shaggy hair. A West African chimp has a paler face than a Central African chimpanzee.

This West African chimp has a pale face.

Where Do Chimpanzees Live?

The place where a living thing lives is its **habitat**. Chimpanzee habitats can be found in 21 African countries. They range from The Gambia in the west to Tanzania in the east.

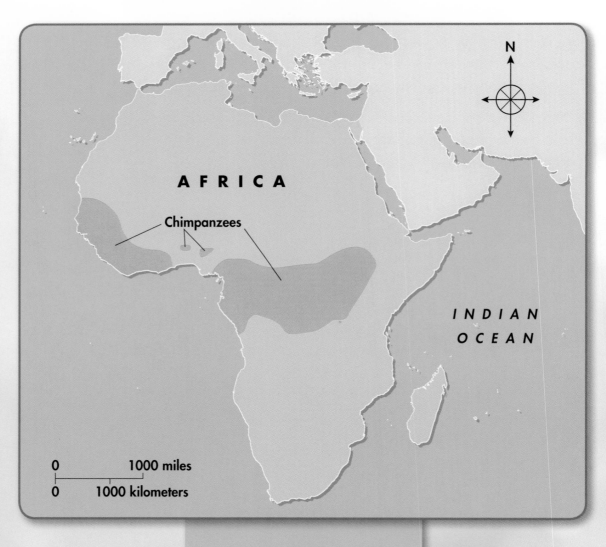

This map shows you where chimpanzees can be found.

Savannahs

Chimps can survive in three different habitats: woodlands, **rain forests**, and flat open spaces called savannahs. This is a wider range of habitats than other great apes, which gives chimps a greater chance of survival.

Chimps do not spend as much time in savannahs as they do in their other habitats. They might wander through a savannah when they move from one area of forest to another. They spend more time in mixed savannahs, which are grasslands with fruit trees. In addition to chimps, many bird **species**, smaller primates, and elephants live in savannahs.

Chimps live on savannahs such as this one in Senegal, West Africa.

Woodlands and rain forests

Most chimpanzees live in densely forested areas such as woodlands and rain forests. Dry woodlands have periods of little or no rain. At other times of the year, they are wet and humid. Chimps have adapted to life in these changing conditions.

Chimpanzees live in these woodlands in Uganda, East Africa.

Woodlands feature many different types of trees and bushes. These supply food for chimpanzees as well as hiding places for many types of animals. In the eastern Congo, there are dense mountain forests. Eastern gorillas, other types of primates, leopards, and okapis live there.

Near the equator lie areas of rain forest. These are humid, densely forested areas. Rain forests are home to an amazing number and variety of living things. In fact, half the animal species in Africa live in rain forests! The rain forests in the Congo Basin in central Africa are the second largest in the world. Chimps in the rain forests of the Congo share their habitat with mandrills, forest elephants, western lowland gorillas, pythons, and many species of bats.

MEDICINAL PLANTS

Many plants in the rain forest can be used to treat diseases or help get rid of ticks. Some chimps have figured out which plants are useful. They use these plants as medicine.

The African forest elephant lives in the Congo Basin.

What Adaptations Help Chimpanzees Survive?

An **adaptation** is something that allows an animal to live in a particular place in a particular way. Chimpanzees have developed adaptations to help them to live in woodlands and **rain forests**.

Arms, thumbs, and toes

Traveling from tree to tree in the forest requires balance and strength. Chimpanzees have long, strong arms to help them swing hand over hand from one tree branch to another. This type of movement is called brachiation. Chimps also have **opposable thumbs** and opposable big toes, which help them to grasp branches tightly. Opposable thumbs also allow chimps to use tools, which most animals cannot do.

Strong arms, opposable thumbs, and opposable big toes help these young chimps to move around in the trees.

Vision

Chimpanzees, like other primates, have eyes that face forward. This means that the view from one eye overlaps with the view from the other eye. This is called binocular vision. It allows chimpanzees to see a three-dimensional (3-D) image, so they can judge the distance from one branch to another. They know exactly when to grasp and when to let go.

Intelligence

Perhaps the most important adaptation a chimp has is its large brain compared to its body size. Chimpanzees use their intelligence to solve problems, such as how to scoop termites out of a nest or open up a hard nut. They learn from one another and cooperate to accomplish tasks. Chimps also have a good memory, which helps them remember where they have found good food.

This chimpanzee is concentrating very hard! It is trying to crack open a nut or seed using a rock.

What Do Chimpanzees Eat?

Food chains show who eats what in a certain **habitat**. For example, cows eat grass, and humans eat cows. Each living thing is an important link in the food chain. When something happens to one link, it affects the entire chain. If the grass were to disappear, what would the cows eat? Without grass, the cows might starve. Then the people who eat cows might starve, too.

Leopard

Chimpanzee

Termites

A **rain forest** food chain shows what chimpanzees eat, and what eats them.

Dead leaves

Food chains only tell part of the story. Many living things eat—or are eaten by—many different things. A food web shows how food chains are linked together. It looks a bit like a spider's web. It might show that cows eat both grass and corn, and that both humans and lions eat cows. In a food web, many things are connected. This shows how all the living things in a habitat depend on one another to survive.

What's on the menu?

Chimps are omnivores, which means they can eat both plants and animals. A chimp's diet mainly consists of seeds, leaves, fruits, and berries. They also eat birds' eggs and chicks, termites, ants, and sometimes even dead animals. They will also sometimes eat bark and flowers. Finding all this food takes up most of a chimp's day.

This East African chimp is munching on a piece of fruit.

Hunting

Chimpanzees sometimes go hunting. They may hunt alone or in a group. Group hunting is often more successful because the chimps can help each other catch their prey. Scientists were surprised to discover that chimps hunt and eat other primates, such as the red colobus monkey. Chimps depend on whatever food they can find in a particular area. If an area has lots of fruit, it may attract groups of monkeys. These monkeys then become prey for chimpanzees. Chimps will also hunt and eat wild pigs and antelope.

Being hunted

Leopards and lions have been known to kill and eat chimps. However, the most dangerous predator of chimpanzees is people. Human beings have killed off more chimps than any other animal in the wild. There are several ways in which humans can cause chimpanzee deaths: by killing them for food, by passing on diseases from which the chimps die, and by destroying chimp habitats. People cut down rain forest trees in order to use the land for farming and to build houses. As their habitats grow smaller, chimps find it harder to find food, and their numbers drop.

HUNTING SKILLS

Scientists have seen chimps hunting with spears in the wild. Fongoli chimps are named after the Fongoli River in southeast Senegal, Africa, because they live near it. They use spears to hunt small primates called bush babies. They stab the bush babies with spears while they sleep, then they eat them.

These chimps have hunted and caught
a wild pig. Now they are sharing a feast.

What Is a Chimpanzee's Life Cycle?

The life cycle of an animal covers its birth to its death and all the different stages in between. Chimpanzees live for a relatively long time. They can live to around 45 years in the wild and around 60 years in captivity.

Group living has benefits when it comes to reproduction (having young). More group members means more options for mating. Chimps mate all year long, not only at a certain time of year. But mating is linked to food sources. More mating takes place when there is plenty of food to eat.

Chimps usually give birth to one baby at a time. They are pregnant for about eight months, just a little shorter than humans. Chimp babies weigh only about 4 pounds (1.8 kilograms). They are helpless and cling to their mothers, much like human babies.

From about six months onward, they ride on their mothers' backs. They do this until they are about two years old. Like all primates, female chimps feed their babies milk from their bodies. Until young chimps are five, they depend on their mothers for food.

Males reach adulthood at 16 years old, and females reach adulthood at 13. This is the time they are able to reproduce (have young of their own). At this time, many female chimps leave their group and join another group of chimps. Males stay with the group they are born into.

CHIMP RESCUE!

In January 2009, hunters and their dogs surprised a Fongoli chimp group in the forest. The chimps ran away and left behind a baby chimp. Luckily, two men rescued the baby, but it needed its mother. A group of scientists flew to Senegal to help. After some searching, they found the chimp's group! Its mother was hurt but alive. They gave the young chimp, Aimee, back to its mother. Soon it was feeding and staying close to her side.

Newborn chimps need their mothers for food and protection, just as newborn humans do.

How Do Chimpanzees Behave?

Chimpanzees are social animals. This means that they like to be with others. They live in groups of about 20 to 100 members. These groups are called communities. In each community there is one **dominant** male. He is the one who decides how to divide up meat from a hunt among the group's members. The rest of the group consists of other males, females, and young chimps.

This young chimpanzee is biting an adult male's finger. It seems odd to us, but this is one way chimps show respect to a dominant male!

A community usually stays within its own area, known as its home range. The size of the range depends on where the chimps live. In certain forests, it may be only a few square miles. In the savannah, it may be hundreds of square miles.

The social lives of chimps

Chimps have as varied a social life as humans. The members of a community will play, fight, bully, make friends, and show tenderness.

Grooming is the chimps' most important social activity. It helps chimps bond with each other and calm down when they are upset. It is also a way to figure out roles in the group. Grooming can be a way to show who is dominant. Males groom each other more often than females do.

Chimps usually get along with members of their own group, but they can sometimes be violent. They may attack other chimps that wander into their range. They are unusual in this respect, as most primates do not band together to kill. In fact, the only other primates that behave this way are humans!

This female chimp is attacking a male chimp. She is trying to protect the baby riding on her back.

Movement

Chimps have different ways to get around. They tend to rely far more on their arms for movement than humans do. They walk using the knuckles of their hands for support against the ground. This is called knuckle-walking. They also swing through the trees from branch to branch using their hands and arms.

A chimpanzee's arms are longer than its legs. This is perfect for knuckle-walking.

Communication

Chimps have many different ways of communicating with each other. They use facial expressions to show their emotions. They open their mouths slightly when they feel relaxed or playful. They pout their lips to beg for food. When they attack, they bare their teeth with their mouths wide open. They also enjoy physical contact with each other such as kissing, tickling, touching hands, and hugging.

Chimps do not talk the way humans do, but they do make noises called vocalizations. The typical chimp sound is a call known as a pant-hoot. Each chimp has its own, unique pant-hoot. Chimps also scream, grunt, roar, and make other sounds. When trying to communicate with a chimp or group far away, chimps may drum on trees. Excited males stamp the ground and scream.

These chimps are pant-hooting.

Studying chimps

Scientists who study primates are called primatologists. They work with chimpanzees in the wild, as well as in zoos and rescue centers. Their work takes a lot of patience. It can be difficult to find a chimp community in the wild. The scientists must be careful not to disturb the community. They will spend many, many hours watching them.

Primatologists take careful notes about what they see the chimpanzees doing. Then, they share their findings with other scientists and the public. They give us a window into the amazing lives of chimpanzees. Because of their work, we know a lot about how chimps behave.

The more we study and understand chimpanzees and their behavior, the better we are able to help and protect them.

JANE GOODALL

Jane Goodall is a primatologist who, in 1960, went to the Gombe area of Tanzania to study chimpanzees.

People did not know much about chimps then. They believed chimps were vegetarians. However, Goodall saw chimps hunting other animals and eating their meat. She also observed them using tools. This was an incredible discovery. Before this, scientists had thought that only humans used tools. People also believed chimps were shy and peaceful like gorillas. Goodall observed that they can be violent and aggressive.

Goodall went on to found the Jane Goodall Institute to continue her research. Today, the Jane Goodall Institute helps to protect chimps as well as study them in the wild.

A DAY IN THE LIFE OF A CHIMPANZEE

A young male chimpanzee lives in a forest in Central Africa. He wakes up at dawn. He spends much of the morning roaming around on the ground and hanging out in trees. He also spends some time looking for food.

Around noon, when the sun is at its hottest, the chimp, along with the rest of his group, takes a break. The group is called a community. Members of the community play, groom one another, and groom themselves. Some of them take a nap. Our chimp finds a tick in his fur. He picks it off and pops it in his mouth. Yum! Does that sound like a tasty snack to you?

Suddenly, an older male drums his feet on the ground. Something has upset him. Our chimp makes sure to stay out of his way!

Most of the feeding takes place in the afternoon. Our chimp finds some ripe berries in a bush. Later, he climbs a tree and munches on some tasty leaves. It can be hard work to find enough food in the forest. His favorite foods are fruits such as bananas, pawpaws, and wild figs. He also likes to dig around in logs for delicious insects or to steal birds' eggs from their nests.

At night, our chimp builds himself a nest to sleep in. He makes it by piling up branches, leaves, and vines high in the treetops. In his nest way up above the ground, he will be safe from other animals that might want to hunt and eat him. He had better get some rest. Tomorrow his community may move on to a new spot.

This chimp is relaxing in its nest high up in the treetops.

How Intelligent Are Chimpanzees?

Chimpanzees are very intelligent. They can solve problems. They observe the world around them and take in information. They have a good memory of the places where they have found food before. They also find new food sources by watching the behavior of birds and other primates.

Like humans, chimpanzees are able to recognize themselves. They have self-awareness. This means that they know that they are separate from the world around them.

Chimps spend a lot of time communicating with each other. A chimp will watch another chimp's face closely to figure out how it is feeling.

Chimps can recognize themselves in a mirror.

Chimpanzees are capable of doing many things that other animals cannot do. In the 1970s, scientists were able to teach some chimps how to use sign language.

Sign language is used by deaf people to communicate with others, by using hand and body movements. Chimps who were taught how to sign could communicate very complex ideas to their human handlers.

The fact that chimps were able to learn sign language shows that they are very intelligent.

SIGN LANGUAGE

In 2003 a professor saw a chimp named Coby using sign language. Coby lived at Black Pine Animal Park in Albion, Indiana, a park for rescued animals. At first the professor did not believe it. Where did the chimp learn to communicate this way? The professor found out that Coby had lived with a human family for his first five years. The family had taught him how to sign. However, no one at the park could understand him. After 2003 Coby began re-learning sign language. Now he is able to communicate with humans again.

Tools

Like humans, chimps have **opposable thumbs**. Having opposable thumbs is important for tool use, because it means that it is possible to grasp things in the hand. This ability helps chimps to do all sorts of things, including using tools, gathering food, grooming one another, and grabbing onto branches and vines. Chimps are among the few kinds of animals that can use tools.

Young chimps learn tool use from watching adult chimps. Then they practice on their own. Many tools are used for hunting and eating food. Chimps in West Africa use stones to smash open nuts. They place the nuts on a flat rock or tree stump. Smashing the hard shell releases the tasty nut meat.

CHIMPANZEE CULTURES

Not all chimp groups use the same tools or use tools in the same way. Each community passes on its own customs to its young. This means that chimpanzees have unique cultures, just as humans do.

Drinking and bathing

Chimps use leaves to scoop up water from rivers or streams. Then they spoon the water into their mouths. Sometimes they use these leaf scoops to get at water deep inside trees. They also use leaves to wipe their mouth and other body parts. All these behaviors are examples of tool use.

Fishing for insects

Both in the wild and in captivity, chimps fish for ants and termites. They use long, thin branches or stalks to poke into ant or termite nests. When they pull out the branch, it is covered with ants. Then they can gobble up this tasty snack!

These chimps are fishing for termites in a termite mound.

What Threats Do Chimpanzees Face?

Chimpanzees are amazing, intelligent animals. Sadly, they are also **endangered** and are at risk of becoming **extinct**. At one time, there were as many as one million chimpanzees in Africa. Today, there may be as few as 150,000 chimps left in the wild.

Risks to chimpanzees

One major reason chimpanzees are dying out is **habitat** loss. People have taken over woodland and **rain forest** areas that were once home to chimps. They cut down the trees and use the land for farming, roads, and houses. This forces chimps to move into new areas or to live in smaller areas. With less land, it is hard for them to find enough food.

Land is often cleared by burning local plant life.

Chimps are also at risk from poaching (illegal hunting). People hunt and trap wild chimpanzees to sell to zoos or as pets. Sometimes people hunt chimps for their meat. The meat of wild animals is called bushmeat. The people who hunt chimps for bushmeat need the money they earn from selling it, and they need to feed their families, too. This makes it a difficult issue to deal with.

Another risk to chimps is disease. Chimpanzees can become sick from some of the same diseases that affect humans, such as HIV and the ebola virus. When people get close to chimp habitats, they can pass on deadly diseases.

In the past, scientists have experimented on chimps. Their similarity to humans made them useful test subjects. Over time, many people began to believe this was wrong. Harming these intelligent creatures seemed cruel. Today, most countries no longer allow experiments on chimpanzees.

This chimp has been taken into captivity.

All dressed up

Chimpanzees are clever and entertaining animals. They look so similar to people that they can be very funny and appealing to us. Some people take advantage of this. They put chimpanzees in live performances, on television, and in movies. They use chimps to sell products. They are sometimes dressed up in human clothing and taught to perform tricks.

Do you think it is funny or cruel to dress chimps up like people and make them perform? Do you think they would be happier back home in a rain forest with their community?

Seeing chimps doing tricks and human tasks may seem funny, but it can be harmful. Chimpanzees can suffer a lot in captivity. They may be kept in chains or small cages. Furthermore, capturing a chimpanzee upsets its community. When a baby chimp is being taken from its group, the other chimps will try to protect it. This often results in many of them being killed.

Close to us, but not human

Chimpanzees share many qualities with humans, but they are not human. They are strong animals that belong in the wild. Only zoos with trained zookeepers and living spaces similar to the chimps' natural habitats should keep chimps. Chimps do not make good pets or entertainers. Treating them like humans can lead to injury—both to chimps and to humans.

THE DANGERS OF CHIMPANZEE PETS

In 2009 a chimpanzee named Travis made headlines for a terrible reason. This adult male chimp lived with its owner, Sandy Herold, in Stamford, Connecticut. One morning Herold was having trouble calming down the chimp. She asked her friend Charla Nash to come over and help her. When Nash arrived, Travis attacked her. Nash lost most of her face and her hands. Years earlier, Travis had been in movies and advertisements. His owner did not imagine that he could possibly be a danger to anyone.

How Can People Help Chimpanzees?

There are many reasons to care about what happens to chimpanzees. They are intelligent animals with complex behaviors. Learning about chimpanzees can teach us much about ourselves. Chimps are an important part of the **ecosystem**.

Jane Goodall Institute

Many organizations are leading the fight to save chimps. Jane Goodall (see page 27) founded the Jane Goodall Institute in 1977. This group works to protect chimpanzees in Africa from **habitat** loss, poaching, and other threats. It also aims to improve understanding and treatment of all great apes. In areas where chimps are hunted for food, the institute helps people find other food sources so they do not have to eat bushmeat. Saving chimps depends on helping the people who live near chimp habitats.

Many organizations are working hard to help chimps like this one.

Bushmeat Crisis Task Force

Another group that fights poaching is the Bushmeat Crisis Task Force. It aims to protect animals at risk from illegal hunting. The task force works with groups to find solutions to poaching. Often this means finding other sources of food for hunters.

Both of these groups work to **conserve** chimp habitats and populations. The message these organizations send is that chimps are worth saving and they *can* be saved.

A TASTE FOR BUSHMEAT

In some areas, bushmeat is prized as a special dish. Logging and mining has led to the building of new roads. These roads lead to areas that used to be hard to reach. Now it is easier for poachers to reach chimpanzees. The result is that bushmeat is growing popular in cities and towns across the world.

This young chimpanzee is clowning around with its keeper in a sanctuary in Zambia, Africa.

What can you do?

There are many things you can do to help save chimpanzees. You can support conservation organizations and write letters to your government about habitat loss. You can write letters or send emails to companies that use chimpanzees in advertisements. Tell them that chimps belong in the wild, not on television selling products. You could refuse to buy these products.

You should also reuse and recycle as many materials as possible. Fewer resources will get used up and the habitats that these resources come from can be saved. You should always recycle old cell phones. They contain a material called coltan, which, when mined, destroys chimp habitats. All these actions help not only chimpanzees, but also all other living **species**, including humans!

Recycling at home helps protect habitats all around the world.

Roots & Shoots

The Jane Goodall Institute runs a program for young people called Roots & Shoots. Children can take action to help the environment and save wildlife. There are tens of thousands of members in nearly 100 countries. The children take part in projects all over the world. Some have sold soup and baked goods to raise money for Roots & Shoots. Others helped zoo workers to expand a bird exhibit.

Learn more

The most important thing you can do to help chimps is learn about them. Share chimpanzee facts with family and friends. Talk to them about why it is important to help protect chimps.

These children are taking part in Jane Goodall's (far right) Roots & Shoots program.

What Does the Future Hold for Chimpanzees?

The future of chimpanzees is uncertain. Chimpanzees are **endangered** and continue to die in large numbers in the wild. Human populations grow and grow, crowding out chimpanzees from their **habitats**. However, there is reason for hope.

Today, many organizations are working hard to save chimps and other primates. Chimps are being born in the wild and in zoos. If their habitats can be saved, there is hope they will live on. Perhaps one day there will once again be a million chimpanzees in Africa.

Each baby chimp born in the wild brings hope for the future.

Wise words

Primatologist Jane Goodall explained how the efforts of young people can make an important difference, saying:

Roots creep underground everywhere and make a firm foundation. Shoots seem very weak, but to reach the light, they can break open brick walls. Imagine that the brick walls are all the problems we have inflicted on our planet. Hundreds of thousands of roots and shoots, hundreds of thousands of young people around the world, can break through these walls. We can change the world.

NEW LIVES

In October 2010, there was reason to celebrate in Gombe National Park in Tanzania. Two female chimps, Bahati and Fanni, had given birth. The babies were born within the area where Jane Goodall began studying chimps 50 years ago. Researchers studied the two young chimpanzees from afar. They seemed healthy, and their mothers were protective. The birth of chimps is always good news.

If we all work hard to protect chimpanzees and their habitats, there is a good chance they will survive.

Chimpanzee Profile

long, strong arms

black or brown
body hair

forward-facing eyes

pale white, pink,
or brown faces

Species: Western chimpanzee

Weight: 70 to 130 pounds (32 to 60 kilograms)

Height: 3 feet to 5 feet, 6 inches (1 to 1.7 meters)

Habitat: Rain forests, woodlands, savannahs

Diet: Seeds, leaves, fruits, berries, birds' eggs and chicks, termites, ants, wild pigs, red colobus monkeys, antelope

Number of young: One infant is born after 8 months of pregnancy. Females will give birth every 3 to 5 years after they have reached maturity at 13 years of age.

Life expectancy: Around 45 years in the wild, and 60 years in captivity

Glossary

adaptation body part or behavior of a living thing that helps it survive in a particular habitat

classify group living things together by their similarities and differences

conserve protect from harm or destruction

DNA basic code for life that is found in each cell in the body

dominant strongest; most powerful

ecosystem community of living things that depend on one another

endangered threatened with extinction

evolve change gradually over time

extinct living thing that has died out

habitat natural environment of a living thing

mammal animal that has fur or hair, gives birth to live young, and feeds its young on milk from the mother

opposable thumb thumb that can face and touch the fingers on the same hand

rain forest forest with tall, thickly growing trees in an area with high rainfall

species group of similar living things that can mate with each other

Find Out More

Books

Goodall, Jane. *My Life with the Chimpanzees*. New York: Pocket Books, 2002.

Moore, Heidi. *Protecting Food Chains: Rain Forest Food Chains*. Chicago: Heinemann Library, 2011.

Solway, Andrew. *Classifying Living Things: Classifying Mammals*. Chicago: Heinemann Library, 2009.

Websites

www.rootsandshoots.org
Visit this website to find out how young people can save chimpanzees.

http://kids.nationalgeographic.com/kids/animals/creaturefeature/chimpanzee/
Learn about chimpanzees at this website, which includes videos.

Organizations to contact

World Wildlife Fund
www.wwf.org
WWF works to protect animals and nature.

Endangered Species International
www.endangeredspeciesinternational.org/index.php
This organization focuses on saving endangered animals.

Center for Great Apes
www.centerforgreatapes.org
This group offers a sanctuary for orangutans and chimpanzees that have been used for entertainment purposes, research, or kept as pets.

Index